SECOND-GENERATION SLAVERY

SECOND-GENERATION SLAVERY

Tale Of A Migrant

ANELECHI BON AGOHA

Copyright © 2021 by Anelechi Bon Agoha.

All rights reserved. No part of this book may be reproduced in any form or by any electronic or mechanical means, including information storage and retrieval systems, without permission in writing from the publisher, except by reviewers, who may quote brief passages in a review.

ISBN: 978-1-957054-03-2 (Paperback Edition)
ISBN: 978-1-957054-04-9 (Hardcover Edition)
ISBN: 978-1-957054-02-5 (E-book Edition)

Book Ordering Information

Phone Number: 315 288-7939 ext. 1000 or 347-901-4920
Email: info@globalsummithouse.com
Global Summit House
www.globalsummithouse.com

Printed in the United States of America

Dedication

My profound tribute to all who suffered and or died in the most terrible and inhuman treatment the world ever witnessed and recorded: The eighteen Igbo slaves of Nigerian descend who drowned themselves in true heroic refusal of being taken into captivity at Dunbar Creek in Simon Island, Georgia; the little 10-year-old Priscilla of Sierra Leone, kidnapped and sold into slavery in South Carolina, as recently revealed by the United States' NBC News Network. Special dedication to people of Biafra region of present-day Nigeria led by Mazi Nnamdi Kanu who are being persecuted like the Israelites of the old by the Government of Nigeria.

I will not forget to mention all immigrants and refugees across the universe who have suffered any kind of oppression, humiliation, intimidation, bullying, torture, and injustice, together with all freedom fighters and all world wild advocates of peace and tranquility. Lastly, I wish to call on the United Nations Office of Human Rights Commission, to please rise to occasion of rescuing mankind from cruelty.

Acknowledgment

To Chris Ohazurume whose prolonged friendly conversation prompted and motivated my candid interest on this topic. Great Mazi Nnamdi Kanu of Indigenous People of Biafra (IPOB), and my adorable children, Pearl Nnenna, Britney Ozichi, and Princeton Chibuike Agoha.

Contents

Dedication i
Acknowledgment iii
Disclaimer vii
Synopsis ix
Summary..xiii

Chapters 1   Slavery In Retrospect................... 1
Chapters 2   Deprived Identity........................ 7
Chapters 3   Religion 17
Chapters 4   Workplace Abuse 28
Chapters 5   The Violated 38
Chapters 6   Integration 46
Chapters 7   Desperado................................ 55
Chapters 8   Human Trafficking................... 67
Chapters 9   Citizenry................................. 72
Chapters 10   Affordable HealthCare 78
Chapters 11   Revenge 86
Chapters 12   Eliminating Slavery.................. 96
Chapters 13   Tribute 100

World Mysteries 106
Authorbiography 109

Disclaimer

This book contains some statements that are graphic.

Reader's discretion advised.

Synopsis

Although slavery is no longer legal in this global world today, an estimated three-quarter of humanity are still trapped in some form of bondage against their will. The history of slavery, a journey of pain and sorrow spans many years, cultures, nationalities, and religions. However, the renaissance of present-day slavery which I call "Second-Generation Slavery" or Volunteered Slavery, orchestrated by present day global migration cannot be over-emphasized of being enhanced, encouraged, and politically motivated and legalized by numerous underlying factors, particularly economic menace as prevalent in most third-world countries.

The Portuguese, followed by British and Americans travelled to the hinterlands of Africa around 1462 with guns and chains to steal, kidnap, rape, extort, export, and sell Africans into slavery, while in present-day dispensation, the Western world has devised and resorted to introduction of enticing and misguiding immigration programs like the United States Diversity Visa Program and other similar programs in Germany, the United Kingdom, France and Canada for example to encourage individuals from all facets of academic and professional levels of life to voluntarily vie for places in these schemes in purchase of their flight tickets on self-accord to engage in volunteered slavery, all in misconceived pursuit of life greener pastures. Human trafficking is yet a more glaring example of second-generation slavery whereby vulnerable, under-aged girls are offered great modeling and acting opportunities in countries like the U.S.A, some parts of other Western world, and the Middle East like United Arab Emirate as now trending, by some international racketeering gangsters in disguise for sexual exploitation jobs or an underworld job nicknamed, 'Work at night, sleep in the day", or "prostitution" as popularly known Worldwide.

In 1865, President Abraham Lincoln ratified the 13th Amendment of the U.S. Constitution, stating, "Neither slavery nor involuntary serfdom shall exist within the United States of America". But little would anyone thought and believed that slavery would still exist in the 21st century on the shores of the United States of America in different forms, levels, and disguises.

In capitalist economic systems, business owners, founders, and operators subject their employees and workers to undue extended, extensive and strenuous hours and days of work, and in some cases unfavorable work conditions and environments for minimal salary compensations, "Peanuts" and other subdued benefits while they wallow in wealth of millions and billions generated by same workers as they compete amongst themselves as millionaires and billionaires as affirmed in an outcry to American people by a two time Democratic Party primaries presidential aspirant, Bernie Sanders, a Senator from Vermont, referencing his proposed legislation to introduced to the Senate on September 5, 2018. But to no avail.

Leaders of African countries and some other underdeveloped third world countries who clinch to untold hardships and deaths to their subjects who see fleeing to various parts of Europe and America as their best surviving option are not exonerated from orchestrating and perpetuating this second-generation slavery.

SECOND- GENERATION SLAVERY

Summary

As much as Slavery seem to have been legally abolished globally today, an estimated three-quarter of humanity are still trapped in some form of bondage against their will. The history of slavery, a journey of pain and sorrow spans many years, cultures, nationalities, and religions. However, the renaissance of present-day slavery which I call "Second-Generation Slavery", or "Volunteered Slavery" orchestrated by present day global migration cannot be over-emphasized of being enhanced, encouraged, and politically motivated and legalized by numerous underlying factors, particularly economic menace as prevalent in most third-world countries. This book goes ahead to reiterate that leaders of African countries and some other underdeveloped third world countries who clinch to powers without meaningful programs to better the lives of their subjects are not exonerated from orchestrating and perpetuating this second-generation slavery against mankind.

ANELECHI BON AGOHA

Chapter One
SLAVERY IN RETROSPECT

MAP OF AFRICA

Slavery recorded in history as journey so harrowing and traumatic without any reparation to date as it began in Africa. Though Atlantic slave trade later abolished in Denmark in 1803, Britain 1807, USA 1808, Netherlands 1814, France, 1814, and Portugal in 1878, the evil trade mostly took advantage of the following ten tribes of Africa.

CHAMBA: The Chamba people, currently known as Samba, Tchamba, Tsamba, Daka and Chamba-Ndagan, are an African ethnic group found in the Gongola State of East-Central Nigeria and neighboring parts of North Cameroon.

WOLOF: The Wolof people are a West African ethnic group found in Northwestern Senegal, The Gambia and Southwestern coastal line of Mauritania. In Senegal, the Wolof are the largest ethnic group, while elsewhere in West Africa they are a minority.

ABRON: The Abron, or Bono, are Akan people of West Africa. They speak the Abron language. In the late sixteenth century, the Abron founded the Gyaaman kingdom as an extension of the Bono state in what is now known as Ghana and Côte d'Ivoire.

FULANIS: The Fula people (or Fulani, Fulani or Fulɓe), numbering between 20 and 25 million people, are one of the largest ethnic groups in the Sahel and West Africa, widely dispersed across the region. They are primarily nomadic Muslims scattered throughout West Africa, from Lake Chad in the east to the Atlantic coast in the west. They are concentrated principally in Nigeria, Mali, Guinea, Cameroon, Senegal, and Niger.

FAN: The Fang people, also known as the Fãn or Pahouin, are a Central African ethnic group found in Equatorial Guinea, northern Gabon, and southern Cameroon.

MANDE: Also known as Mandinka, Mali, or Mandingo group of peoples of Western Africa, whose various Mande languages form a branch of the modern-day Niger-Congo language family. Mande people are primarily agriculturists, and most are full-time subsistence farmers.

BAKONGO: They live along the Atlantic coast of Central Africa, in a region that by the 15th century was a centralized and well-organized Kongo kingdom but is now a part of three countries. Their highest concentrations are found south of Pointe-Noire in the Republic of Congo, Southwest of Pool Malebo and west of the Kwango River in the Democratic Republic of Congo, and

North of Luanda, Angola. They are the largest ethnic group in the Democratic Republic of Congo, and one of the major ethnic groups in the other two countries they are found in.

YORUBA: Also known as Àwon omo Yorùbá (Children of Yoruba'), the Yoruba are an ethnic group of Southwestern and North-Central Nigeria, as well as Southern and Central Benin. Together, these regions are known as Yorubaland. Majority of this tribe is from Nigeria, and the Yoruba make up 21% of the Nigeria's population, making them one of the largest ethnic groups in Africa, per Nigeria's projected population.

MBUNDU: The Mbundu, also known as Northern Mbundu or Ambundu, are a Bantu-speaking people living in Angola's North-West, north of the Kwanza River. They are distinct from the Southern Mbundu and Ovimbundu people. The Ambundu today live in the region stretching to the East from Angola's capital city of Luanda. They are predominantly in the Bengo and Malanje provinces and in neighboring parts of the Cuanza Norte and Cuanza Sul provinces.

THE IGBO: The Igbo people are an ethnic group native to the present-day south-central and southeastern Nigeria. Geographically, the Igbo homeland is divided into two unequal sections by the Niger River – an eastern and a western section. The Igbo are also one of the largest ethnic groups in Africa.

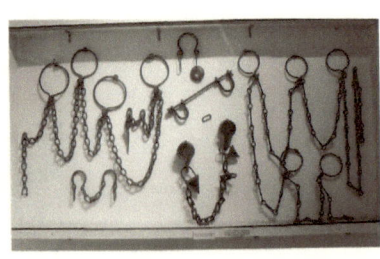

Photos by:
Obinna Kelvin Anukam

Chapter Two
DEPRIVED IDENTITY

It is not merely the physical part of slavery and bondage that makes it cruel, degrading and dehumanizing, but also the arresting of free thought, deprived identity, and the acknowledgment of its contribution to society. Africans and citizens of other war-torn and mismanaged countries of the World are committing suicide by fleeing from their countries of origin. Running away is obviously seen as last resort to seeking freedom and a promising future. People, especially school-age young adults, were once allowed to apply for student visa to travel abroad from Nigeria for instance to study in colleges and universities in the United Kingdom and the United States only in areas of studies that were domestically unavailable, not anymore. The functionalities of local colleges and universities are presently questionable. Families with financial capabilities are only left the option of shipping their wards outside the shores of Nigeria for their academic pursuits. Lack of available employment opportunities for the teeming graduates in the country makes returning to Nigeria a nightmare and encourages remaining in foreign countries of studies for employment and greener pastures which requires strenuous processes to normalize their stay that turns them into unforeseen and accidental immigrants. Most importantly, one must not forget those teeming jobless graduates presently fleeing to different parts of Europe, America, and other parts of the world within their reach in search of opportunities. Tens of thousands of those fleeing have unfortunately perished enroot their intended destinations through drowning by seas, heatstroke, and dehydration in the deserts, and in various other ways, while others are forced into slavery as reported to be taking place in some parts of Libya by the Cable News Network (CNN) in one of its investigative coverages, shortly followed by then United Nations Secretary-General, Antonio Gutierrez's brief and direct to the point public appeal speech: "I am horrified at news reports and video footage showing African migrants in Libya reportedly being sold as slaves. I abhor these appalling acts and call upon all component authorities to investigate the said activities without delay and to bring the perpetrators to justice, accordingly. And I ask the relevant United Nations actors to actively pursue this matter. Slavery has no place in our world and these actions are among the egregious abuses of human rights and may amount to crimes against humanity. I urge every nation to adopt and apply the UN convention against transnational organized crime and its protocol on trafficking in persons and I urge the international community to unite in fighting this scourge. And this also reminds us of the need to address migration flows in comprehensive and humane manner through development cooperation aiming at addressing its root causes through a meaningful increase of all the opportunities for legal migration and through an enhanced international cooperation in cracking down on human smugglers and traffickers and protecting the rights of their victims".

Even at the end of all these ordeals, the very insignificant percentage that make it to the so-called promised land must settle for menial jobs that subject them to working almost every available hour like robots for their survival and comfort to barely making ends meet.

Let us put color aside. What is the difference between an average white man and average black man? Geneticists prove all human races arise from the same ancestral lineage. But contrarily, every other race feels superior to black people and vice versa. Excuse me to say, a white trash homeless and drug addict on the street feels superior to every black person that comes his or her way. It is given that the poor and uneducated Africans are the most hard-working Africans; they are seen selling merchandize on the hot sunny streets of African towns and cities and crushing stones in the villages of Africa, while the African intellectuals are nowhere to be found as they cannot invent a simple water filter to purify water or stone crusher to increase stone crushing to commercial quantities. African governments, politicians and leaders cannot finance and sponsor projects to encourage and create jobs. Africans both at home and diaspora are only good at articulating their certificates and degrees without actualizing them into realities mainly due to lack of facilities, grants, and sponsorships.

So long as you depend on a white man's inventions and fly a white man's plane without manufacturing one, particularly not being able to maintain and manage an operational and functional flight business operations as is the case with Nigeria despite her teeming educated and skilled population scattered all over the world, the white man must feel and remains superior to you, and possibly demean you to their delight.

As President Paul Kagame of Rwanda states, "We need to mobilize the right mindsets, rather than more funding. After all, in Africa, we have everything we need in real terms. Whatever is lacking, we have the means to acquire yet we remain mentally married to the idea that nothing can get moving without external finances. We are even begging for things we already have. This is absolutely a 'Mindset' Failure".

Nigeria for instance has not understood the value of cross training its citizens in its three major languages of Igbo, Hausa, and Yoruba. Rather, Nigerian leadership with shire sentiments and stupidity of purpose imposes Arabic language in its school curriculum system for some selfish religious pursuit and aggrandizement. Some of the senseless African politicians are stupendously empowering their youths with bikes and other petty items of lesser value, while their counterparts in other developed countries are investing in education, science, technology and infrastructures of meaningful development and advancements. Also, Nigerian politicians have their children scattered all over the world at the best colleges and universities that money can afford while they travel to better equipped, better staffed, and well-maintained health care facilities and hospitals in Dubai, Europe, and America for their medical treatments while their subjects are left with facilities of much lesser accreditations in their country. At one time, the president of Nigeria himself spent about six months in Europe on a stretch and continuously visited same for medical treatments without even relinquishing his position. Wow! What a country of hopelessness. The insensitivity of African politicians in a whole is unabated and unprecedented. It is unimaginable that Nigeria imports petroleum while crude oil is being locally extracted within its shores. Nigeria imports rice and beans despite huge plots of untapped and untamed virgin lands to her advantage. How else can a people undermine and sabotage themselves and their country without decorum?

Second-Generation Slavery

In my humble opinion, Nigeria lost its great God-given opportunity to technological advancement, especially in gears and warfare wares with its maltreatment and self-destructive mishandling of the Biafran team of renowned Bazooka and Ogbunigwe manufacturers right after the Civil War in their failure to assemble and keep them together for continuity just shire arrogancy and lack of patriotism. What an expensive and irreparable mistake!

Nigeria is the most populous country in Africa with almost 200 million people straddling both sides of the Niger River. The country is nearly equally divided in terms of religion with about 60% of Christians and 40% of Muslims. Nigeria, amongst other her natural mineral resources, has Africa's largest oil deposits with about 20 billion of the 66 billion barrels of proven oil reserves in all of Africa along with 3 trillion cubic meters of natural gas. But surprisingly, Nigeria suffers as one of the worst poverties in the entire world to date. Why would a country so rich in natural resources suffer so greatly? The answer lies primarily in who controls Nigerian oil reserves: International companies like Shell and Chevron who have being exploiting Nigeria for decades due to Nigerian leaders selling their souls to the devil in their zealous desperate war deal to conquer Biafra during the Civil War of 1967. Exxon's exploitation and royalty payments into the ruling family's private accounts in Equatorial Guinea provides another example. It is preposterous that a President wins about 96% of general votes cast in every presidential election held in the country for over thirty years. Is this still regarded as democracy or as a hijacked democracy, if not flat-out tyranny?

African politicians in general, and Nigerian politicians particularly are crooks stealing the future of their subjects.

Without being overly judgmental, I tend to support or concur to a school of thought that states, "African politicians and leaders have sold their souls to the devil, and they have some special place so reserved for them in hell". Indeed, their insensitivity to issues of importance and necessity lean towards yet another school of thought that states, "There's discrimination in creation as evident in African politicians' reasoning, lack of objectivity, vision, initiative, and patriotism compared to other ethnic leaders."

In all fairness, in utter disregard to entrepreneurship, blacks all over the world have perpetually subjected themselves to abject slavery to the slave masters and colonial masters. Take American professional football for instance which is made up of about 70% black players, both retired and active, without any franchises owned and managed by blacks or African Americans. The issue with quarterback Colin Kaepernick who up to this time of my writing is assumed to have been kicked out of the league as punishment to being outspoken against unfair treatment, injustice, and systemic racism in a claimed system of equity and justice of the United States of America.

During the 2018 FIFA World Cup Soccer Tournament, a sarcastic social media article drew unprecedented attention of the World in saying, "France, 'The select African team' are 2018 FIFA World Cup Champions". Out of France's twenty-three players, fourteen were of African descent. African descendants, who would have represented their various ancestral mother lands, rather ended up representing the Whiteman who was responsible for their ill and inhumane treatment of slavery. Imagine when African team countries represented by Egypt, Morocco, Nigeria, Senegal and Tunisia couldn't qualify for round of sixteen, a lot of notable African players of different generations were still in the tournament representing majority of other countries' teams like England, France, Belgium, Portugal, Denmark and a host of other countries far into the tournament though their immense contributions to their various teams' successes were undermined intentionally by the press and sports commentators of same foreign countries they represented. Pertinent to say, it is pathetic turn of events that Africans dominated the 2018 FIFA World Cup Tournament representing countries of other continents. And in my fair assessment I stand to say, DIVERSITY won! INTEGRATION won! MIGRATION led by Africans won the 2018 FIFA World Cup!

Chapter Three
Religion

For all the continuous miscues, the question, did Africans yield to pressure and critics of the colonial masters to give up on, or abandon their god(s) or ancestral god given as religion remains one of the world's greatest mysteries today as it is obvious fact that almost every other race like Asia, India, Middle East, and others have or adopts different religion akin to them, but the black race? Speaking on ancestral gods, it's my wish to state that I am not and till eternity will never be an advocate of neither wooden nor metal carved gods (Man-Made gods) in any form and manner, but notable for instance is, Egbu-Owerri of Nigeria, my ancestral root and birth place then undoubtedly identified with "Amadioha", God of Thunder" and "Otamiri", River Goddess in connection with Egbu being the main source of Otamiri river, and both being unseen or invisible, and non-man-made. Very spiritually effective, loving, caring, and protective, but punitive dependent on prevailing circumstances as history and our forefathers disclosed to us. In their era, community subjects had respected the rules, laws, regulations, and elders. They had loved, cherished, and respected one another in ordinance of Amadioha and Otamiri Egbu as they were popularly referenced. So, why are they no longer of any significance? Was it by coincidence or calculated logistic target that Egbu-Owerri with such great traditional and community strong history and ancestral connection became one of the major hubs of the then early Christian Missionaries, the Anglican Missionary Society Fellowship precisely chose as a hub to spread their missionary gospel in the entire Southern part of Nigeria or Igbo land that led to the translation of the English Holy Bible to Igbo language as carried out in Egbu as history reveals?

The Holy Bible refers to Almighty God, Jehovah, "The unseen, omni present and omni silent God of the Israelis". The question remains, where is the God of Africans (Amadioha)? Will it be true to say that just as Israelis' God (Jehovah Yahweh) got angry with Moses His chosen and beloved prophet and leader of the Israelites at a time, (Deuteronomy 32: 51-52), as God declared with reasons that Moses was not permitted and must not enter the Promised Land: Jehovah Yahweh got angry and told Moses, "You broke faith with me in the presence of the Israelites at the waters of Meribath Kadesh in the Desert of Zin and because you did not uphold my holiness among the Israelites, therefore, you will see the land only from a distance; you will not enter the land I am giving to the people of Israel"- (Numbers 20:1012) God told Moses and Aaron that, because they failed to trust Him enough to honor Him as Holy, they would not bring the children of Israel into the Promised land. God rendered punitive judgement in not allowing Moses to get into the promised land. Would one be out of place to say that Africans are suffering same or similar as Moses from African ancestral God who must have gotten angry with Africans for abandoning Him in their observance of a foreign religion as introduced to them by the Whiteman?

May I also humbly employ you to google, "Origin of Male Circumcision" to see for yourself that in relation to Genesis, (Gen. 17), God told then Abram to circumcise himself, his household, and his slaves as everlasting covenant in their flesh. Behold, history has the same act of circumcision to have originated in Eastern Africa long before Abram's era. This's to say that a known focal ritual of Africans adheres to date already put them in the right path to proper life and spiritual doctrines with Ofor na Ogu" as their guiding life principles but letting go due to the caprices of the white man that came with missionary political, and commercial agenda hidden under the disguise of religion remains a mystery. Did African forefathers fall short and abandoned their already compliance to life religious rituals as provided by their ancestorial God with lack of common thinking that the creator of life created differing faces, races, creed, and backgrounds just like differing talents and gifts of nature assigned to every one of us, allowing us to differently stick to our own, per our different races for a reason and purpose, hence differing methods of worship media? "If aren't broken, don't fix it", as Americans would say. How could Africans as a race adapt, embrace, and be so fixated to a religion that never recognized them, their culture, and traditions as a people from Genesis to Revelation, except in negative encounter with Pharaoh and his Egyptians, (Book of Exodus of the Old Testament of the Holy Bible) and the Ethiopian Eunuch, (Acts 8:27) and (Isaiah 53:7-8…39), a school of thought so questioned?

With good behavior and dedication, Africans are loved, cherished, and nurtured just like a stepchild to his or her adopted parents, but priority is on the biological child.

Then comes the big question, are African ancestral God(s) angry with Africans for neglect, abandonment, and disobedience, hence put a spell on them? A spell of non-performance and excellence even amid plenty as synonymous with black race leaders and Nations? The truth may not be farfetched.

Following available records and data, Christianity- (much of New Testament of the Holy Bible seem to be revolutionary version of Judaism- (much of the Old Testament), the older, main, and official religion of Israelites, (God's Chosen), which outstanding percentage of Israelis has refused to succumb to or adopt with their rejection of Jesus Christ as Messiah as they maintained their worship system of Judaism is generally and officially identified with Israelis and not Christianity. Religiously and otherwise, we are all aware of "Content" being the key and successful life principle. And if so, why didn't African forefathers stick to their own for there must have been reason(s) nature assigned them with their own from inception as is the case with our individually assigned talents and gifts of life?

I pray that God abide in us as we endeavor tracing right perspectives without being tagged blasphemous.

The question of polygamy is yet another interesting one. The Bible nowhere explicitly condemns it. The first instance of polygamy in the Bible was that of Lamech in Genesis 4:19: "Lamech married two women." And Several prominent personalities in the Old Testament of the Holy Bible like Abraham, Jacob, David, Solomon, and others all had multiple wives, and in some cases concubines (Girl Friends or Side Chicks). Then comes the big question, why did God allow polygamy, but Christianity as introduced to us by the Whiteman condemns it? Polygamy is a denied culture by the Whiteman which is evident of the Islamic world's reason resisting Whiteman's infiltration and so-called civilization into their natural and polygamous culture as is the case with the Whiteman and his introduced Christianity that is contrary to the Old Testament of the Bible. Reality of life reveals that while men by nature are so insatiable with just one woman as synonymous and obvious in animal kingdom with packs or herds of multiple females and their cubs or babies headed by or led by a male as rightly practiced in the Islamic world and some other parts of the world in abject resistance to Western World's condemnation of it over Monogamy as created by the Whiteman that is only best and advantageous for economic reasons as evident in present day economic challenges and dispensations. Polygamy as a viable and natural cultural phenomenon of Africans as a people must be encouraged than condemned or eradicated to avert yet another evil plot to undermine African culture and lifestyle.

Identifying some confusions and possible mysteries life avails Africans, suffice it to say, "slavery destroyed us, while organized religion (Christianity and Islam) divided us unequivocally" as a people.

Furthermore, religious wars for instance have claimed millions of lives undeniably, turned millions homeless, and created the greatest enmities amongst mankind. Stating, Chinese have been in existence 2070 years before Christ. The first history of Japan was 210 years before Christ. The Koreans have been existing 2333 years before Christ. History also has it that Indians were dated as far back as 3300 years before Christ. Our Lord Jesus Christ was born in AD1, (Anno Domini), and He died in AD 30/33 as history recorded. While Prophet Muhammed (PBUH) was born on 570 CE, (Common Era). That was 570 years after Christ, and he died in 632 CE.

In line with the above, the following are the resultant questions and concerns we as people of this world seeking solutions to mysteries of religion are faced and challenged to:

    a. Is there any given prove that for all the thousands of years the Asians and Indians existed before Christ, they never heard of God, and God left them to exist in the world created by God?

    b. Why did the Holy Bible, the Quran, and other scriptures sourced from the

Jewish and Arab Nations of worship never mentioned anything pertaining the Asians and Indians who history tells us were already in existence, prior.

c. Why is the history of mankind narrated in the two (Holy Bible and Quran) religious books and scriptures only covered the Jewish and the Arab nations, exclusively?

d. As we assume and probably agree that the Whites and the Blacks are true generations of Adam and Eve because of our looks, but why did the Holy Bible and Quran not explain where the Chinese, the Japanese, the Koreans, and the Indians originated from?

e. Why is it that the two religions that claim to be the most holy in the world that were generated by two sons of same lineage, Abraham the most divisive religions, causing unrest and most hatred among their followers and the rest of the world?

We must as a matter of facts agree that it is obvious that the Christians are Christians because they have faith in a certain prophet, book, and scriptures. The Muslims are Muslims because of their believe in a particular prophet, book, and principles. Jews are Jews as well because of their religious believe akin to them. The Buddhists are Buddhists because of their sole believe in their own way of worship, and so is every other people of different ethnicities, creed, and possibly colors of the world. As can be derived, there is no evidence to support any theory that God intends a single religion for the entire world or that God intends to grant paradise to any religion as it may be reasonable to assert that every individual shall be judged according to their faith and deed on Earth. Per my perception, the world will become a peaceful place only if we can grant freedom of religion and worship to all for life's only certainty is death. The Jews will die, the Christians will die, the Muslims will as well die, just as the Buddhists and atheists will die.

Therefore, brothers and sisters of the world, is it worthy killing ourselves for religion, especially those who erroneously and misguidedly believe in destruction of other peoples' lives and properties to attain Martyr status or for hilarious reward of unbelievable 7000 virgins in paradise? May we all, please give peace a chance to help restore world stability and minimize migration. After all, from all perspectives stated above, every individual or group religion practice settles to be predominantly by birth location based, rather than it is on individual choices at birth. Hence, all religions must be allowed to be practiced and co-exist parallel to each other.

Chapter Four
WORKPLACE ABUSE

The African immigrant population in the United States of America has tripled in the past two decades, per analysis of census data conducted by Queens College, New York. Communities of Nigeria, (The most populous African Nation), Ghana, Ethiopia, Eritrea, Kenya, Senegal, and others are constantly taking root in urban American enclaves and suburbs. By the year 2000, foreign-born blacks were recorded to constitute 30 percent of the black population in New York City, 28 percent of black population in Boston, about a quarter in Montgomery County and more in Prince George's County of Maryland.

This is the wave of new African immigrants transforming the African American identity. No longer will people assume that all blacks in America have a shared past with slavery or affinity for soul food. As part of the African diaspora, there is a shared challenge to colonial powers and racism, though nuances prevail.

Nigerians in the United States has about 50 percent with bachelor's degrees. According to the 2000 census, African immigrants are more educated than any other native-born ethnic groups, including white Americans, holding twice as many degrees as white Americans and four times as many as native-born African Americans. Though, they face more issues of underemployment, job-age discrimination, and unable to secure befitting job status they were used to at home countries; hence, we have, "Doctorate degree holders driving cab" situations amongst them as it is known.

Pertinent to state that the 1986 Immigration Reform and Control Act of the United States of America made it easier for undocumented immigrants in the United States to become permanent residents. In 1990, the Diversity Visa Program was introduced. As part of the 1990 Immigration Act, this program was designed to promote immigration from under-represented countries outside the United States of America to migrate to the United States to up to about fifty thousand Africans annually. Africans who come to the United States are here to work so they can provide for their families at their home countries in Africa. Some of them fled political and undue ethnic persecution as is presently the case in Nigeria where the Fulani Jihadists led by the president, President Buhari and his Cabals are stopping at nothing in trying to run down Southerners of the country, especially the Igbos in their utter intent of total Islamization of the whole country, while some fled due to tribal wars and other untold maladministration tendencies of their leaders. Eventually, when they get here, they work after acquiring their education as they find out they cannot go back home as there are no job opportunities at home, so they stay abroad indefinitely. This puts them in to being disguised slave workers in their newfound foreign land.

A black American or African American friend narrated her recent encounter with assumed, "Inquisitive" sub-urban white American colleague of hers at one of their lunch outings who asked her, "What's the difference between being 'Black' and being 'African American'?" My friend stated she responded, "Good, some people feel 'African

American' has more of a cultural identity." She adds, "It can also refer to blacks with long time roots in America, versus if your roots are elsewhere."

"What do you mean? Her colleague countered!

"For example, if you're talking about African American culture, that term refers to maybe the experiences of slavery and the culture that emerged after it." "Versus if you just migrated from Nigeria for example, she continued. If you are Nigerian, obviously you are African American. You're black and live in this American country, but culturally, at first you may have strong ties to Nigeria as bad as it may sound and would prefer 'Nigerian American'".

"But both are still blacks, right?" he asked!

"Well, yeah! But the culture they emerged from is different as it is. So, it just depends on what you may be talking about culturally. If it is about Soul food, and Blues, you must be talking about African American culture. And if you are talking about Pounded Yam, Egusi, Efo-riro, Edikiko, Jeloff

Rice, Vegetable Soup, Yam- Porridge, Nkwobii and a host of their others, you are talking about Nigerian American." Yeah! That is the truth, and it is what it is!

And as my dear friend rehashed the logic a couple more times, her white colleague got more confused than ever. And in summary, she said, "Black refers to everyone who's black, while African American refers specifically to blacks in the United States of America. Black comprises a lot of cultures, and African American seem to be one of them."

As already indicated, Nigerians are amongst the top nationalists with the highest percentage of educated and professional immigrants in the U.S., yet there is no matching transformation of such to inventions and developmental achievements, particularly to home country. Despite some biased, jealous, internal rancor, non-result oriented, and non-achieving community associations headed by some myopic and unscrupulous individuals, Nigerians in diaspora have failed to put their acts together to achieving any meaningful projects that could be taken back to home country development. Though given that majority has profusely complained that the crop of obnoxious, selfish, and never do well home-based politicians and leaders will stop at nothing to unleash their evils against any ideas and systems being introduced from outside poised to denying them of their usual crude source of ill wealth acquisition. It must be déjà vu of their unrefined system, otherwise they will declare and render it nonconforming and nonfunctional system or idea.

As previously stated, migration can be driven by a richer country's doing, as well as a poorer country's doing or undoing. Not too long ago in Nigeria, an enterprising young man appeared to have it all. He was the head of energy research for a Pan-African bank in Lagos, Nigeria's biggest city, had a healthy (and growing) amount of savings and investments, and ran an e-commerce business on the side. Then came this so-called opportunity, he resigned and moved with his young family to Canada, eventually getting a job as an investment associate in a wealth-management firm in Calgary. His previous employer in Lagos promoted someone to replace him soon after, but, like him, the new employee quit as well and moved to Calgary. This time, rather than search for another replacement, the bank disbanded the energy-research team. In some ways, such story is not unusual: a skilled professional leave a job at home in search of work in wealthier parts of the world, betting that the short-term instability of uprooting an established life will be worth it in the long term. Nigeria ranks in the top 10 in terms of the number of skilled workers leaving for Canada over the past five years. The sparsely populated North American country has long been a favored destination of immigrants around the world because it offers economic opportunities, a strong safety net, and a diverse population. Many of these immigrants have been drawn by a tweak to Canadian immigration rules. In 2015, Canada implemented a new system for taking in skilled immigrants, using a points-based calculation in which applicants are scored on the bases of their age, work experience, education level, and language skills. It aims to prioritize those who are most skilled and ease their entry into the country, while encouraging applicants to settle in less populated parts of Canada. Not to mention that Australia and New Zealand use similar systems, and British Prime Minister, Boris Johnson has also said he wants to implement one, too.

In effect, then, one would gladly say, thanks to a tweak to an immigration system in richer countries, developing ones have suffered serious consequences, loosing skilled professionals- many of whom are highly educated and would be expected to make outsize contributions to a state's economy, tax income, and society more broadly like the Nigerian Dr. Onyeama Ogbuagu, who was at the core of developing the much-needed vaccine for the United States government for the mighty COVID-19 of recent. In Nigeria particularly, the conveyor belt of young talents that are supposed to replace those who are emigrating is whirring slowly, and the impact is apparent: The country's educational institutions groan under the weight incessant strikes by underpaid staff protesting poor funding and outdated infrastructure; medical procedures are regularly delayed due to shortage of specialists; and companies are even closing entire departments to cope with frequent staff exits. What is now Africa's largest economy is no stranger to the departure of its best talents. Pertinent to mention that in the 1970s and '80s, skilled and semi-skilled Nigerians were recorded to have left the country, mostly for the United States, Britain, and elsewhere in Europe, fleeing the rule of successive military juntas and economic mismanagement. A 2010 report by the Migration Policy Institute, a Washington, DC based think tank, found that by the late 1970s, about 30,000 Nigerian professionals had graduated from universities and colleges in the United Kingdom but never returned to Nigeria; by the mid '80s, 10,000 Nigerians were in the United States, many of them highly skilled. This brain drain had a knock-on effect that opened a route for these immigrants' relatives to leave Nigeria as well joining their loved ones and families.

A close African American friend of mine had asked, "why can't African leaders make our mother-land enticing for us to find reasons to find our roots back to Africa?" Very impressive question! Why can't our leaders make Home-Africa habitable, comfortable, and possibly inviting with simple infrastructures and developmental enhancements to encourage our kits and kin taken into slave captivity to want to come back home after being let free by abolition of slavery? Rather, due to instability and lack of opportunities, we are still voluntarily migrating to the slave masters to enslave ourselves also to those who took advantage of our dear people and brought unimaginable hardships to our race. This is Second-Generation Slavery. This is Volunteered Slavery.

Chapter Five

THE VIOLATED

This notable nation of the continent of Africa with one of the best and recorded both natural and human resources a country can boost of on the planet earth whose seed of discord and disunity was sown by a crooked British North and South amalgamation program of the country in 1914, followed yet by her first population census that was manipulated to favor the Northern part of the country that remains to be corrected that has so embedded internal wrangling, maladministration and non-performance of leaders that has trickled down to under development and lack of improvements in all facets of economic development, resulting to lack of gainful employment opportunities to all levels. Hence, making offshore traveling of its teeming population to all parts of the world the best option to survival as is the case with numerous other third world countries.

In line with the afore mentioned trend, little did it take after graduation for Amber who graduated top of her class from one of the newly established tertiary institutions of the South-South part of the country winning the latest released U.S. Diversity Immigration Visa Lottery to move to the United States Of America or "Amiricaa" as is commonly referred to by locals, making her parents to borrow, pledge, and possibly sell as much personal properties as they could to enable their daughter travel to the U.S.A. which is seen as chance to grip of hard currency as is the case with other known families in and around the neighborhood.

Shortly after Amber's arrival and normalizing her immigration status, she was able to secure a job with the help of alumni at Burger Kings (BK) Restaurant. Being a personality, you may not miss to identify, little did it take McNeil who was a regular to this restaurant due to proximity of it to his bank office located adjacent to the Burger King Restaurant to develop keen interest on Amber. And while Amber was occupying one of the cash registers on this faithful day, McNeil had a very rear opportunity to slip his business cards to her, requesting her to give him a call for a possible job opportunity in his bank office. In Amber's follow up calls, McNeil offered her a job position as Bank teller in his branch's next hiring exercise after realizing in couple of their phone discussions of Amber's finishing top of her class back in Nigeria that even sealed her chance and better cover up for McNeil in offering her a job position despite being a fresh immigrant in the country.

Shortly after Amber's one year anniversary as employee of this noble bank, McNeil made Amber a backup Vault Key Holder with every backing reasons he could find available to buttress his reasons and argument to his managers, including and not limited to; Amber has an impeccable dressing habit and good personality that makes her stand out and needs to be encouraged to grow with this bank as an under lying incentive to a young and up and coming potential the bank needs.

But little did this young up and coming lady realize that McNeil's kind gestures have a looming undisclosed and none negotiated price tag attached to it. Enroot to executing his ulterior motive, McNeil embarked on yet a different kind disguised gestures to humble and intimidate Amber who already see him as angel with granting her a quick promotion to back up Vault Key Holder as he started inviting her to his office for purported counseling on false allegations from customers and even her colleagues and peers of Amber's raw and thick accent that makes it difficult, if not impossible for her to be heard and understood clearly; an intimation and humiliation ploy commonly used by most complex Americans both on the streets and corporate settings in execution of their vicious acts. Though, promising her, "Not to worry, I will take care of those as long as am still the boss here". And in another development, Amber and her Alumni, former co-worker, Chuka had gradually started expanding their work place relationship rules and regulations' held back interest for each other which now is no effect following Amber's transition to a bank worker in line with Chuka's constant push and advances towards that in as much as Amber who has a very strong family background routed in the principles and doctrines of devout Anglican Church Christianity denomination, here in the U.S. known as Episcopal Church with her father so dedicated to his belief that he is taking classes enroot to being ordained a Reverend Pastor back at home in Africa. And

Amber who has remained celibate long since after her brief relationship run with a boyfriend in her freshman year in the University and planned on remaining so for the right man was contemplating on how best to handle Chuka's advances, praying and being hopeful that he would comprehend her plight so to say with appreciation to give them a chance to take their intended relationship grow when started. But unfortunately to unsuspecting Amber who was invited to a seat down drink on this faithful day was taken aback and rapped by McNeil at this designated guest house not too far from their work location and his onslaught subsequently continued on a regular quickie bases inside the Vault room on work pretentious maneuvering as she could not voice out or speak to anyone about this malicious acts of McNeil as a new overwhelmed and naïve immigrant who doesn't want to lose her so called bank job she sees as professional status-quo elevation by all standards against being a Burger King Sales Person and most importantly, has no knowledge of her rights to protect herself against predators like McNeil as she languished in agony of McNeil's violation of her and all her beliefs and future womanhood plan of dignity.

He carried out his onslaught to Amber on a self-urged time basis. Per her faith and belief, each time McNeil broke all border protocols to enter her republic, her holy land, Amber felt defiled; she felt unclean and unholy for she is daughter of "African Holy Man". She felt grain of sewage being flushed into her system as she is being violated by such filthy, shameless, disgusting, and godless evil man of not her specs and choice. It made her feel like animal defecating on her.

Though the initial pains and discomfort surfaced as expected and disappeared after the first unconsented eating of her apple by McNeil being her first time after a long period of abstinence, but now came back with more intense pain and discomfort after about a month and half. And on her way back from work on this day, she stopped by CVS Pharmaceutical Store to purchase a self-test pregnancy test kit to, according to her help her eliminate her worst unthinkable nightmare of being pregnant. But, contrary to her least expectations, the result came out positive. The beautiful innocent, naive, reserved, and unsuspecting Amber, violated by McNeil is now with pregnancy of out of wedlock to a "happily married" man, McNeil. Tormented with anger, frustration and disappointed with herself and God as she questioned, 'God, why and how would you let such evil befall your own?", "God, what must I do for abortion is not an option" continually all through the night, crying and weeping nonstop through the night without a wimp of sleep. She endlessly blamed herself for not taking protective measures, for letting procrastination take greater part of her that resulted to this ugly situation. God Lord, this is unwarranted, why would you let your people suffer such fate? She questioned and lamented in vain! She questioned herself if she had opportunity of reporting McNeil's evil act at the beginning would have helped stopped this?

She could not wait for daybreak; the next morning, she headed to work with eyes swollen and turned red as if she were in a WWF wrestling fight the previous night with a hand-written note she managed to scribble on a sticker. On getting to her office, her first port of stop was her immediate Supervisor's office with the excuse that she was just informed of an immediate family emergency and would like to take the day off to enable her attend to the issue. And just as she had planned it out, pretended leaving out the door, she quickly made a U-turn and headed to McNeil's office to thunderously slip her hand-written note of emergency to him that reads:

It is critical that you see me as soon as today as a matter of urgency. Just call me when you are on your way, with her address and phone number following the short note and she immediately dashed out of his office and out of the building, disappearing into thin air without waiting for him, McNeil to say, "Jack"!

(#WhyIDidntReport)
(#BelieveSurvivors) (#METOO)

Chapter Six
INTEGRATION

In fair need to talk about race amongst all, a suburban Montgomery County, bordering Washington, DC the Nation's capital, hosts this state's largest public-school system. While the county is generally known to be affluent, it is increasingly racially, culturally, linguistically, and economically mixed. Its public schools enroll more than150, 000 in 200 schools across nearly 500 square miles of the county. Its students come from more than 157 countries with more than 138 languages. The public-school officials in this county have long nurtured and promoted the system's reputation for rigorous academic programs, college-bound high school graduates, and stellar achievement. Over the past decade, students of color here have become the majority, and the share of students from families that earn low incomes has also grown. And as is true in so many other increasingly diverse suburban districts, about 80 percent of Montgomery County teachers are whites. Pertinent to mention that in late 2014, the county's school superintendent, Joshua Starr announced plans to initiate a recruitment drive specifically designed to increase the racial and ethnic diversity of the county's teaching force. And amid the demographic changes, administrators adopted some ambitious program that starts with a seemingly simple act: people from a variety of racial and cultural backgrounds sit in a circle to talk. The Study Circles Program, as it was called started in 2003, organizes and facilitates group conversations at schools for students, parents, and educators, usually with the help of Landesman, a school coordinator in the county school system and his colleagues. Since the year 2004, the county schools have hosted more than seven hundred study circles which are mainly convened usually only if staff members have requested for it. The goals are straightforward: to spur discussion about the ways racial and cultural experiences play out in the county school system's classrooms, cafeterias, and even in the hallways. How they permeate the learning experience for kids, their effects on teaching practices, and their impact on decision making and policy making amongst adults. The Circle members explore a variety of questions, including: Are students of color treated differently from white students? What are teachers' assumptions about why kids act a certain way or why they do not excel? How might adult expectations, unconscious biases, or lack of understanding of students' cultures and experiences set up barriers to students' educational achievements? How might we remove those said barriers?

Per Landesman, "Ultimately, what I hope is that the status quo isn't right." The hope, too, is that the study circle participants will collaborate on some action plans to improve policies and practices or resolve conflicts they identify together. And after developing a shared understanding of a problem, many past and present study circle members do construct these action plans to present their concerns and ideas to school leaders. In recent years, parents and teachers have addressed such challenges as making enrollment in gifted and talented programs better reflect the demographics of a school, hiring more bilingual staff members, and training bus drivers who parents had perceived as being disrespectful to students.

About 63 percent of Montgomery County students are students of color as recorded, with Latino students the most numerous (about 27%). Latino kindergarteners and first graders represent about 30.7 percent of students in these grades in Montgomery County, just slightly outnumbering white students in those early years of schooling. A little more than a third of students come from families with low annual income that they qualify for free and reduced-price school lunch, even though it is still one of the nation's wealthiest counties, with a 2012 median household combined annual income of about Ninety-five thousand dollars ($95,000).

In April 2014, a report from the Montgomery County Council's Office of Legislative Oversight detailed increasing racial and economic segregation in the county's high schools. The report also noted a widening gap in achievements between white students and students of color. So, even as officials attempt to build relationships and focus on equity on the schools that are becoming more diverse, worsening segregation may very much threaten equity and cross-cultural understanding and interactions in this growing school system. Recent research has indeed shown that socioeconomic integration is strongly associated with improved achievements. In a 2010 study for the RAND Corporation, researcher Heather Schwartz found that students from low income earning families who went to schools with lower levels of poverty performed much better over time than their counterparts who attended schools with higher poverty rates, even when per-pupil spending in the higher-poverty schools was $2,000 higher than in the lower-poverty schools, following a deliberate effort to provide more resources to high-poverty schools. Schwartz found that about two-thirds of this effect was due to students having been in a lower-poverty school. The other third of the beneficial effect, she said was due to students living in a lower-poverty neighborhood, via an inclusionary zoning program of the county that encourages construction of affordable housing.

In their 2013 book Confronting Suburban Poverty in America, Elizabeth Kneebone and Alan Berube of the Brookings Institution reports that during the 2000s, more jobs and more people at a variety of income levels moved to Montgomery County, and up until the middle of decade, the poverty rate dropped slightly. However, they find that no other county in the Washington, DC., region, including District of Columbia experienced increase in poverty of the same magnitude during the late 2000s. Specifically, the county lost seven thousand jobs since 2007. The number of residents living below the poverty line surged by two-thirds, with more than thirty thousand people now officially poor.

In 1990, immigrants accounted for less than one in five county residents. By 2010, one-third of county residents were immigrants and more than 40 percent of the foreign-born lived-in poverty. Nearly all the growth in the county's labor force of about 96 percent is attributed to immigrants according to the state-government-created Maryland Council for New Americans. Jobs created in a booming economy attracted immigrants at both ends of the wealth and education level continuum. As the Maryland Council for New Americans reports, more-educated immigrants, who tend to come from India and other Southeast Asian countries found work in technology and science industries. Immigrants with less formal education filled numerous lower-wage service-sector jobs in hotels and restaurants, as nannies and landscapers, and in construction. El Salvador in Central America is the most common country of origin for immigrants in this county, Montgomery. It is also recorded that immigrants from Vietnam and

Sub-Saharan Africa has as well established identifiable and growing communities in this Montgomery County.

The overall signature achievement of former Montgomery County school superintendent Jerry Weast, who hired Landesman to launch the Study Circle Program, was a systemic and very public focus on the disparities in opportunities and achievements between schools in wealthy, large white 'up county" communities and poorer, racially mixed "down county" communities such as Silver Spring which borders Washington, DC. Weast's efforts are detailed in the book, leading for Equity: "The Pursuit of Excellence in Montgomery County Schools."

It is, therefore, pertinent that we look at the data and ask ourselves the hard questions, says Tomas Rivera-Figueroa, assistant principal at Parkland Middle School, one of the "down county" schools where the leadership team spent two days in a study circle ". Our building has 45 percent Latino students", Rivera-Figueroa says. "Why is it that 95 percent have a 2.0 GPA?" And even though 25 percent of the students are African Americans, "why is it that most of suspensions are African American?"

"The kids are the first to say, 'The teacher doesn't understand me'" says Rivera-Figueroa, who has been Parkland's assistant principal for nine years. "We have to have those conversations and create an understanding."

Parkland as observed offers a textbook case of the changing American suburban school. Its study circle also demonstrates that creating a more inclusive, fair, and successful school will require purposeful steady work. Students of Color-African American, Hispanic, and Asian children make up about 85 percent of the student body. While the principal is Asian, and the assistant principal is Latino, the school staff by contrast is 70 percent white.

A UCLA Civil Rights Project of 2008 report

reveals that African American and Latino teachers were far more likely than white teachers to report that they had "quite a bit" or 'a great deal" of training in any methods designed for racially and culturally diverse classrooms. About 60percent of Latino teachers, 58 percent of black teachers, and 70 percent of mixed-race teachers reported these amounts of training, compared to only 42 percent of white teachers, according to the study. (Susan E. Eaton – Integration Nation of 2016)

Chapter Seven

Desperado

America, 'Land of the free and home of the brave". The Holy Bible, "For the Lord your God is bringing you into a good land; a land with streams and pools of water, with springs flowing in the valleys and hills; a land with wheat and barley, vines and fig-trees, pomegranates, olive oil and honey; a land where the bread will not be scarce, and you will lack nothing; a land where the rocks are iron, and you can dig copper out of the hills". Deuteronomy 8:7-9.

So, arrived a young family from North-West of Nigeria led by their father, Vincent and mother, Mercy with their two-little young ones of five and seven years old as new immigrants settling in Takoma Park of NW, Washington, DC.

Vincent and Mercy got married shortly after their National Youth Service Corp Program at

Owerri, capital of Imo State where they served together as new graduates' couple of years back to proceed in having two beautiful children in quick successions, prior to running into the opportunity of travelling to the United States of America for greener pastures. Back in Nigeria, Vincent worked as a staff of privately owned Oil Service Company in Port Harcourt, the capital city of River State as Accountant, being a graduate of Finance out of the University. While his wife, Mercy, whose area of studies was History, got a Middle High School teaching job in one of Port Harcourt's City School system.

Vincent and his family were blessed to be accommodated by a Good Samaritan spirited family friend's Three Bedroom Town House on arrival. Hence, allowing him ample time to financially be able to save for their residential accommodation. But as time as so gone past about nine months that they were still a guest at this friend's residence, Vincent was desperately looking for job to independently sustain his family and possibly secure accommodation for them as their welcome into their friend's house was being overstayed. Though Vincent was engaged in Pizza delivery work he was only able to do with their host's 2009 Toyota Corolla car on his off days and sometimes after his return from work on a part time bases pending when a good and steady income job opens or become available. As disparate as he was, Vincent was ready, available, and determined to get started with whatever becomes available as steady and guaranteed income job to enable him plan better for his family moving forward without being dependent on their host. Hence, comes this Chauffeur position job he applied for couple of months ago to become the personal Chauffeur to the President and CEO of a Company based in Washington, DC as specified in the job description after his two-failed job hunt attempts with both PNC Bank and Giant Grocery Store, both located in the neighboring suburban town of Silver Spring.

Vincent had never had to worry of his experience or whether he would succeed in coming across as brilliant as he want, till his last unsuccessful job interviews. Today, dressed in a scrip blue double-breasted suit, his intent to impress this Chief Executive was a bit of a worry. As good as it may be, he could do nothing but think about it for time is of the essence for him and his family to move on without soiling the good relationship with their kind and benevolent host, Andy.

"Good morning", he said to the middle-aged white female Secretary-Receptionist as he entered the main lobby of this six Story building housing Prinzimo LLC and some other businesses in same location through the glass revolving door.

"My name is Vincent Preyee. I am here to meet with Mr. Dennison. Mr. Dave Dennison". He is the president and CEO of Prinzimo LLC.

May I see your ID, the Secretary requested? Vincent quickly pulled out his ID which he had positioned in his shirt's breast pocket for easy access in one of his preparing moves to help eliminate nervousness. She took it, examined it to verify name, looked up at his face, smiled and handed it back to him. Then, made a brief phone call directed him to the elevator to take him to the 6th floor to Mr. Dennison's office floor.

As he walked out of the elevator on the 6th floor to get into Mr. Dennison's office as directed by a stand-by female staffer, he observed a lounging section to the left in this large office space with two brown leather couch and oak tree coffee table, a big book shelve stacked with lots of books and journals to the right side of the office and then sitting in the center was an executive desk with a black reclining chair for the executive with two black leather armchairs for visitors right in front of the executive desk.

"Good morning, Sir", Vincent Said, while almost prostrating.

"Have a seat" Mr. Dennison said without much lifting his eyes to Vincent's face. Vincent quickly hurried to one of the armchairs as he pulled his half-paged resume from his folder and placed it in front of Mr. Dennison's seat, incredibly careful as not to disarrange the layers of papers and journals strewn across his desk in a jumble.

"Okay Mr. …., allow me to call you by your first name, Vincent, Mr. Dennison said, while placing the resume down in front of him and leaning back in his comfort chair. "Briefly tell me about yourself",

Vincent immediately perks up. This seem to be the question he had looked up, mastered, and memorized as one of the formidable questions in job interviews.

"Okay Sir," he replied. "As you may have already known my name, I originally hail from Nigeria, West Africa from where I migrated with my family to the U.S. Since my arrival, I have engaged in some other petty jobs but has constantly in delivery services all over the city which much gave the opportunity to master the city pretty much in terms of driving and navigating in and around the city. Hence, why I am suitable and confident with the Chauffeur job position I am here for."

"I see."

"Thank you", he said with quivering voice and not even being sure of what Mr. Dennison was thankful for.

"What is your immigration status here in the U.S.?"

He adjusted himself by seating up a little on

his chair as he beamed with a subdued smile in response," I have my Employment Authorization papers as required by Department of Homeland Security for any migrant to legally work in the country."

"What's that? Mr. Dennison questioned"

"It is a work permit, Sir', Vincent reiterated. "It gives me the authorization to legally engage in job employments until the arrival of my Green Card".

"I see", how long will it take for you to get the Green Card? Mr. Dennison asked.

"Am not very sure really, but this work permit allows me to work until the Green Card is out. It means I am very legal to work, Sir.

Vincent could not continue his eye contact with Mr. Dennison at this moment as he was caught in nervousness and eagerness on this topic, he knows could be a deal-breaker for any new job seeking migrant. How could he have stated the very obvious that this his work permit and even the Driver's License that is key to this Chauffeur job position is so dependent and valid on approval of his asylum application, him and his family being an asylum seekers from Benue State of Nigeria where the Fulani Herdsmen and even Terrorist group, Boko Haram have subdued the citizens and locals with incessant attacks and killings without the intervention and, or protection of the government of the country led by Mohammed Buhari, a Fulani Nigerian.

"Good. I understand your legality and that matters a lot to the process."

"Do you by any means have any outstanding tickets you need to get resolved?" Mr. Dave Dennison asked.

"No Sir", Vincent replied.

"Have you been in any sort of accidents within the last five years, despite who was at fault?"

"No Sir".

Mr. Dennison picked up the resume. One could see and feel beads of sweat rising out of Vincent's forehead.

Vincent could not help it, but to go for a rescue as he pulled a white handkerchief from his pants pocket to dab his forehead to avoid embarrassing himself from excessive sweat. He then took a deep breath as he closely watches Mr. Dennison scan through his resume with keen interest.

"I am a terribly busy CEO, and you will have to know that I'll be your main priority in your job performance. And when Am out of town, you are not in any way on break or vacation. You will rather be with my family as to help them catch up with their needed errands. I don't expect anything short of high performance, integrity and accountability from you." "Most importantly, this position you're seeking comes with a lot of ability to handle and treat confidential and secret matters as such, as you may be previewed to coming across matters of such classifications, do you understand what that means?"

'Very much so Sir. I sincerely give my words,

Sir. I understand that very much being a past student of Finance and Accounting and haven worked as accounting personnel, I know the essence of confidentiality in workplaces, especially as it patterns to the boss."

"Good. You will be required to sign our Company Confidentiality Agreement prior to assuming duties," Mr. Dennison stated.

'Yes, I will be glad to", Vincent responded.

'Do you have any questions for me on all we talked about and, or any other issues of importance or concerns to you?"

"No Sir, you have told me all I need to know, but if any other questions pop up in my thought, I hope you wouldn't mind my bringing them up later? And I very much appreciate your details to all those, Sir."

"Very good, I have got one more interview to conduct this afternoon, before I make a decision. So, you will likely be hearing from me through the

Secretary before the end business day, tomorrow", Mr. Dennison stated.

"Thank you, Sir. I very much appreciate this chance and your time to meet with me personally."

The boss, Mr. Dennison stood up, indicating end of the interview session.

Vincent quickly followed suit. As he tried to straighten his tie, which over the period of the session had tilted.

"That reminds me, Mr. Dennison said, if you're the chosen candidate in this process, you'll be needed to have a better suit than what you have on now, please". And those will be passed on to you later by the Secretary when the job offer will be made."

"Certainly, yes Sir." Thank you!

Mr. Dennison extended his hand to shake him prior to his leaving out of his office with some pronounced beaming smiles and murmuring something in his half turning posture as he walked out, like he was saying, "Thank you and thank God", in feeling that confident that the outcome must be a good one.

Chapter Eight
HUMAN TRAFFICKING

Shocking phenomenal of human trafficking, particularly as they are conveniently carried out unabated in line to addressing the second-generation slavery of this book as outlined in my introduction and highlight cannot be overemphasized.

In 2012, The National Center for Missing and Exploited Children has on record that about 325,000 children are at risk of becoming victims of sexual exploitation in the U.S.

In 2014, buying a child for sex online can be just as easy as selling your old couch or posting an updated resume.

Astonishing statistics dug up by Thorn, an agency that studies technology's role in sex trafficking, found that sites like Craigslist are often used as tools for conducting business within the industry. Incredibly, 70 percent of child sex trafficking survivors surveyed by Thorn were at some point sold online.

"People are posted and sold online multiple times a day," Asia, a survivor of sex trafficking, told Thorn. "As far as the ad that was posted up just like you can go find a car, there was a picture, and a description, and a price."

At least 105,000 children in the U.S. are being sexually exploited, according to the Department of Justice and the National Center for Missing and Exploited Children, and the expanding underground industry has no intent of slowing down. The FBI considers sex trafficking the fastest-growing organized crime, and online channels allowing for the exploitation are only making it easier for predators to do business. NPR reported in March that the Justice Department believes child sex trafficking could generate a staggering $32 billion a year.

Many times, pimps work as expert manipulators to start young people in the business, promising a relationship and wealth. Tina Frundt, who founded Courtney's House in 2008 to protect children from sex trafficking, wrote on Women's Funding Network about her experience with a coercive man who played a role in her abuse.

To Frundt, abusers are dangerous because of their misleading and misguided supportive displays.

"This is the same man that took me out to eat," Frundt wrote on the website. "He listened to me when I wanted to complain about my parents, gave me words of advice and courage to move on." What a gimmick to establish trust?

In Bangladesh for instance, Whenever Bangladeshi brothel owner Rokeya, 50, signs up a new sex worker, she gives her a course of steroid drugs often used to fatten cattle. For older sex workers, tablets work well, said Rokeya, but for younger girls of 12 to 14 -- who are normally sold to the brothel by their families -- injections are more effective. (Getty)

New York City Council member Melissa

Mark-Viverito used a stack of children's shoes as a symbol for child sex trafficking, during a protest rally outside the Village Voice on Thursday, March 29, 2012, in New York in a coalition of religious and civic leaders protest demanding that the Village Voice stop running their adult classified section. The protesters say the section is being used by sex traffickers peddling underage prostitutes. (The AP)

In England, a newspaper advertising board outside a corner shop in the Lancashire town of Rochdale, England, displays, "after nine men were arrested for child sexual exploitation on Jan. 11, 2011. Greater Manchester Police arrested nine men as part of an investigation into sexual exploitation and questioned them on suspicion of rape, inciting child prostitution, allowing premises to be used for prostitution and sexual activity with a child. (Photo credit: Christopher Furlong/Getty Images)

Firefighters help rescue a prostitute after she became trapped in a tunnel from an offensive against human trafficking at the Super Frontera bar late on April 21, 2012, in Guatemala City.

(Photo credit: Johan Ordonez/AFP/Getty Images)

United Kingdom, Undated handout composite image issued Tuesday May 8, 2012, by Greater Manchester Police showing eight of the nine men who have been convicted for luring girls as young as 13-years old into sexual encounters using alcohol and drugs, top row left to right, Abdul Rauf, Hamid Safi, Mohammed Sajid and Abdul Aziz, and with Bottom row left to right, Abdul Qayyum, Adil Khan, Mohammed Amin and Kabeer Hassan. The nine men aged between 22 and 59 were convicted of charges including rape, assault, sex trafficking and conspiracy to be sentenced Wednesday May 9, 2012, at court in Liverpool, England. (AP Photo / Greater Manchester Police)

Chinese police raided and caught a massage parlor with a group of massage girls suspected of prostitution during a June 21, 2011, raid in Beijing, part of a vice crackdown in stamping out deep- rooted official graft. (Getty)

Chapter Nine

CITIZENRY

According to old Greek's founders and supporters of democracy, there are three kinds of people established in any given society:

The Idiot – The idiot is not in any way someone who is mentally deficient. Rather, the idiot is a totally private person, totally selfish and totally self-centered. The idiot is always out for his personal gains at any given time and purpose. He does not have a public philosophy, no knowledge, inept, no character and no virtues to be able to contribute to and be part of a flourishing society and community. He is all out for his personal pleasures and his personal treasures. The idiot, as the Greeks said is just an upgraded barbarian.

The Tribes' People- The idiot the Greeks said is followed by a second kind of people or persons they called the Tribes' People. The tribes' people they said does not mean they belong to certain tribe(s), which is a good thing. But when they use the word "Tribe", they explained that to be people with tribalistic mentality. The tribes' people are those who are not able to think beyond their small tribes or small groups. For the tribes' people, their primary, only, and ultimate allegiance is to their tribe. Their tribe is their guide and their religion tribalistic. They are always afraid and indifferent to things that are novel and different to their old ways and known system. They are always suspicious and fearful, and they always deal with different people and different situations with intimidations, force, and violence. The ideal example of tribes' people are the warriors of the old because they are war making and war creating people.

The Citizens – Finally, the ancient Greek people came up with the third kind of people they called, "The Citizens People", or "The Ideal People". This group of people they stated are not just citizenship status people known in our present-day citizenry or status quo. These they said are people with skills and knowledge to live a public life; they can live a life of civility. The Citizen recognizes that he or she is a member of the Commonwealth and therefore strives for common good for all. The citizen knows his or her rights in the society and as well as responsibilities to the society they belong. The citizen can fight for his or her rights, but always with awareness and respect of the rights and interests of others or neighbors or the smallest minorities, and the worst of their enemies. It is the citizens, they said makeup civilized societies because citizens settle their differences with civility, so they produce civilized society; a society that truly lives up to the true meaning of society. Society literally means friendship and friendliness.

The choice of the above stated kinds of people is the choice dilemma African leaders and politicians are faced with. Would African leaders continue being IDIOTS who only live for themselves? Would they continue being TRIBES' people who are unable to think beyond their small groups or tribes' people? Or would they wake up from their slumber to smell the coffee, realizing that being citizens people is the best and only way out of abject economic poverty they plunged their subjects into, and to help elevate their situations with all the natural resources abound within their nocks and cranny to better living and life expectancies?

By my assessment, the Croatian president, Kolinda Grabar Kitarovic who created storm by her beauty, commitment and selfless support to her national team as seen and recorded in just concluded 2018 FIFA World Cup Tournament in Russia. Born on April 29, 1968. She is a graduate of English and Spanish Literature who did her post-graduate studies in International Relations. She is a Fulbright Scholar who studied at George Washington University, Harvard, and John Hopkins Universities. At the age of 46, in the year 2015, she became Croatian President while pursuing her Doctorate Degree in International Relations. Do not just get waylaid by her beauty because she is an-army commando and an ace marksman too. From 2007 to 2011, she served as ambassador of Croatia to the U.S. Then, she became the first woman to become NATO Assistant Secretary General for public diplomacy. In the NATO Circle, she is known as a "No Nonsense Woman". She instilled discipline and dedication, leading by her own examples. She has been voluminously praised by both Presidents

George Bush Jr. and Barack Obama of the United States of America. Imagine her purchasing her own economy class flight ticket to fly to Russia to witness Croatia Championship game with France, spotting Croatia jersey? She fluently speaks Croatia, English, Spanish, and Danish languages. Moreover, she is so adept in speaking German, French, Russia, and Italian languages. This is an epitome of what a nation's leader should be, falling into the Citizen kind of people. Spotted with Croatian jersey shaking hands and hugging not only Croatian players, but also opposing France players drenched in rain, in true spirit of sportsmanship the game is truly about. Also pertinent to mention is what Ghana presently has in President Nana Akufo-Addo who is well educated and experienced per previous positions he held in Ghana that were vital to his preparation and readiness to ascending the leadership of his country. Amongst his good leadership attributes, Akufo-Addo takes to the streets of Accra in disguise to monitor and check on the utterances and activities of the city police force that has been of public concern regarding their undue ruthlessness in use of force and unauthorized demand of gratifications, which I personally see and regard as selfless leadership with purpose. He is a good example of African Citizen Person of this generation who needs being applauded.

Chapter Ten

AFFORDABLE HEALTHCARE

For a free world America, one would have thought and expected free, complete, and comprehensive health care for the citizens, especially for the hard worked and retired elderly, not the lazy, dead-beat, never employed, and welfare dependent. But not at all, my people.

We must never fall short of the obvious that you are naturally sick and down in health once you are no longer physically able to take care of your daily essential chores and necessities. Hence, you are dependent and needs as much support as possible. Saying, health care is not only about medications and visitations to hospitals and Doctors' clinics, rather boarding and home care inclusive in comprehensive health care, otherwise one will be enslaved to work more than necessary to provide for this life necessity required for sustenance in the later days or years when they are of most important. Our hope and aspirations in the twenty-first century for least is that we survive to a healthy old age, and lead independent lives, passing as we would like and giving our affection and desired attention to our loved ones without strings attached. While the other developed countries of the world systems like neighboring Canada and most parts of Europe help make this hope a reality, the American health care system often shackles people into relationship of dependency in the contrary.

In the United States for example, Medicare helps those aged sixty-five and older pay for their healthcare. But the truth of the matter remains that there are some overwhelming holes in long-term elder care that Medicare doesn't cover like the room and boarding in nursing homes or assisted-living facilities, twenty-four-hour nurse services, home health aides who deliver meals, help bathe the elderly, get groceries, and clean the house. It's absurd to know that the cost of all such services is simply left to the burden of the elderly themselves until they've exhausted all their assets to become destitute. To pay for all the above mentioned in the United States, a conventional wisdom tells us that you need to have saved a million dollars to the minimum before retirement. But based on a 2013 estimate, the medium financial net worth of an average American household headed by someone nearing retirement was, excluding homes, and cars, not much over sixty thousand dollars. Stating, most Americans are nowhere close to meeting the minimum they need. And if they completely run out of finances in old age, Medicaid, the state-run health program for the poor may kick in with often requiring the elderly relocating to a nursing home or facility of probable questionable quality for qualification criteria. It has been observed that some States are even cutting their Medicaid funding and changing eligibility requirements, hence leaving people who once relied on the program to their mercies.

On the inception of Obamacare at the beginning of 2014, some people in Europe had the impression that America's health-care system had eventually been rebuilt. Though Obamacare tried to do something simple and legitimate in providing health care for all, Obamacare happened to be a ridiculously complex, inefficient, annoying, and fundamentally compromised way of trying to do something simple.

Now that there is the Affordable Care Act. From the perspective of Europeans, the State of American health care has been such a strange anachronism so to say for so long as it is reasonable to assume that it should have been fixed by now. Unfortunately, it has not. This Affordable-Care Act did address some of the problems at hand. It has extended coverage to millions of Americans, required insurance policies to cover more people now than previously, and put some limits on insured spend cap. But the law did not make it simple to buy insurances, nor did it address the overall problems associated with skyrocketing costs.

Setting aside the political influence of the private health care industry, are there any legitimate reasons why this United States cannot accomplish what most other wealthy industrial nations of the world has successfully done and done so well, a true public health-care system for its citizens?

The experiences of other successful nations' health care suggest that there is no good reason the United States cannot switch to their similar approach to offer high-quality health care for less costs to its' teeming population. The craving citizens' Universal health care could start in varieties of ways as has been suggested by various public opinions. Both federal and state could operate public insurance plans on the new health exchanges. Medicare for all plans could offer a transparent and fair benefit package to anyone who wants to buy it, and as these plans grow in participation, they could negotiate better and with prices and providers. Suffice to say that some states and counties are now taking matters into their own hands. Vermont is about adopting the Canadian-style single-payer option, for instance.

"America, a typical case of all that glitters that are not gold". Every modern advanced nation of the world like Britain, Germany, France, Canada, and the list goes on and beyond your imagination provide their citizens with free healthcare or affordable healthcare. Why not and why can't our so-called free world, America? It is difficult for Americans to realize what they are missing. Europeans can feel enormously proud and even patriotic about their healthcare systems because they pay for them with their taxes, and they genuinely feel that the system has been created by them and for them. If the system is not working, they are fierce in their critics and their demands for change. Success in creating an excellent public health-care system is on a par with any other great national achievement, whether winning Olympic gold medals or landing a man on the moon. Such pride is within reach, especially since public healthcare seems to be what most Americans, particularly the younger generation or millenniums want for themselves. According to the Pew Research Center, more than half of millennials of this greatest nation on the surface of Earth, believe it's the federal government's responsibility to make sure all Americans have health-care coverage, and there's no reason as great as making it happen, sooner than later in line with as already stated above in my synopsis in which Senator Bernie Sanders of Vermont and 2016 Democratic Party primaries presidential aspirant recently lamented on saying, "The American people at this time of massive income and wealth inequality are sick and tired of having to subsidize profitable corporations owned by some of the wealthiest people in this country. Let me give you a few examples of what I mean; Jeff Bezos, the major owner of Amazon is the wealthiest person on Earth, he is worth about

$155 billion dollars. In fact, since the beginning of this year, 2018 his wealth has increased by about $260 million every single day. Meanwhile, Bezos continues to pay many thousands of his Amazon employees' wages that are so low that they are forced to depend on taxpayer-funded programs such as food stamps, Medicaid, and subsidized housing to survive. Do you know who pays for those programs? You do! But it is not just Amazon. The Walton family of Walmart and many other billionaire-owned large and profitable companies enrich themselves because they get taxpayers to subsidize their inadequate wages. The working families and middle class of this country should not have to subsidize the wealthiest people in the United States of America. That is so absurd. That is what a rigged economy is all about. The fact is that if employers in this country simply paid workers a living wage, taxpayers would save about $150 billion a year on federal assistance programs, and millions of workers would be able to live in dignity and security. Frankly, I do not believe that ordinary Americans should be subsidizing the wealthiest people in the world because they pay their employees inadequate wages. That is why I am introducing legislation on September 5th to demand that Mr. Bezos, the Walton family of Walmart, and other billionaires get off welfare and start paying their employees living wages. Our legislation gives large, profitable employers choice: Pay workers living wage or pay for the public assistance programs your low-wage workers are forced to rely upon. The greed of the billionaire class is having horrendous impact upon our economy and the moral fabrics of this country. Together, we're going to change that."

Chapter Eleven

REVENGE

A special day marks the birth of Leroy by Daniela, a single mother of Dominican Republic Island immigrant who dated yet a student immigrant of Cameroun descends, Larry. Larry had left back to his home country shortly after graduation from a university to try finding a possible job position in his country if situations permit but met his demise after two years of blending in when he felt sick of Typhoid Fever and could not survive of it. Hence, leaving Daniela his Dominican Republic fiancée back in the U.S.A. with its' hustling and bustling as Daniela devastated with the unfortunate development and other family challenges both in the U.S. and back home in the Dominican Republic took to and got stuck to home care and house cleaning job just to make ends meet with his only son, Leroy in his infancy and being kindly and specially consoled and comforted by the 2nd generation Johnson family she was working for on a part time bases provided her with her little Leroy a residence as they moved in and she converted working for them to a live in home care person especially with Mrs. Jackie Johnson, wife to Mr. Gilbert Johnson being diagnosed with breast cancer and bed ridden with her illness. Daniela who now duals her duties as both cleaner and live-in home care giver in helping Jackie with her ill health.

Daniela serving Gilbert and Jackie Johnson family together with their only Teenage son, Chad while nurturing his little boy, Leroy had no reason of looking elsewhere for other job opportunities as she felt blended with the Johnsons till Jackie passed of her cancer couple of years after and Chad who is now of age after graduating from College and obtaining a good job career with one of the Fortune 500 Companies in Washington, Dc as a Senior Procurement Officer commuting from his family country side home of Maryland.

Daniela, a piece of beautiful black Dominican woman with long slender shapely pair of legs that ejected from what could be described as most incredible piece of ass rarely seen without searching with small waist that made her better described as "Figure 8". Her good look that was not fully explored by Larry her ex-Fiancée prior to traveling back to the Cameroun and only fed to a son, Leroy was almost full and standing firm. Although she found herself in such economic situation for a fault not of hers, but share mismanagement of affairs by leaders of her home country, she was very beautiful and her beauty was so engaging that it smote young adult, Chad who had being secretly admiring her that led to his groping and grabbing her from behind on one occasion as she stooped down in her effort to helping Mr. Gilbert Johnson dress up with fixing his shoes to have his way into her after some unavailing struggles and pleading for her submission to Chad that really began continuous intermittent and occasional repeat performance of same act till unknowingly to both, were spotted and caught in the act ensuing after several non-result protracted struggles with Chad as she grew sick of Chad's continuous ambush by unsuspecting Leroy who shockingly filled with anger and furious retreated and ran back to the two bed room quarters allotted to his mom by the Johnsons she occupies with him. He locked himself up in his room in overwhelming anger, rage and with strange bad feelings to do Chad some harm but could not.

Years passed by so quickly leading to up grown of Leroy. His mother observed how much he had grown so tall, strong, muscular, and handsome just like his late father, Larry. One could see he has certain magnetic kind of power of a man like that of the Mandingo of the old African strong man ladies of this generation claymore for and wish their men possess. Leroy had graduated from High School and engaging in some available odd jobs, with Chad now moving his aging father, Gilbert Johnson who had developed some sort of dementia to a nearby Nursing Home where Daniela goes on a daily bases to take care of him while the Nursing and Medical staff take care of his medical needs leading to Chad's remodeling and renovating of his parent's house to suit his generation taste, especially regarding his getting married to his old off and on College Sweetheart girlfriend, Brenda.

Brenda stands out as a beautiful blond girl by all standards with particularly good frame on a height of about 5ft 9ins with moderate pair of breasts and butts together with some set of bright white teeth that qualifies her for any tooth paste commercial you may think of. Her smiles are so contagious and welcoming that one could easily be lured and seduced by it.

With youthful exuberance and exploiting tendencies, the Mandingo boy, Leroy carried out his known exploration on a young neighborhood Latino girl, Marie. Marie was about two years older than Leroy and a class ahead of him in their senior high school, though it was hard to tell. Both had a little close call and couple of intermittent interactions in recent past, and with that Leroy felt time was right to take this not well-established neighborhood friendship to another level when he followed Marie to a nearby park for a chat. Leroy with his aggressive tendencies quickly thought of getting into seductive discussions with Marie shortly after their initial exchange of pleasantries by admiring her long dark curly hair and oblong face which she acknowledged with appreciations of not realizing Leroy to be that observant and detailing in his description of a young lady as much he did. Marie instead of responding to Leroy's too invading comments and questions that followed excused herself for a pee and requested Leroy to please keep an eye on any on-coming person or intruder as she rushed into a small nearby bush. But, instead of watching as had been asked to, Leroy turned to a peeping Tom of no effect as Marie emerged shortly after. And with a short and brief kiss to the mouth by Marie's house entrance door as he walked her home, they called it off for that evening to what seem to have initiated the boy-girl next door neighborhood relationship.

Shortly after Brenda's arrival to the Johnsons as Chad's wife, he called in Daniela and her son, Leroy for a formal introduction and to request that domestic help and other assistances as may deem fit be extended to Brenda as and when needed. Over time and unknowing to anyone else, Brenda who had in most of her adult life lived, worked, and socialized in New York with its great diversity and happens to be color blind as she had even dated some Asian American Restaurant Owner in the past in New York is now secretly admiring young Leroy with his physical appearances that tend to so much overshadow his young age to give him the look of early thirties in age. With this new secret development progressing, on this day as Leroy was mowing the backyard lawn with Brenda relaxing with a drink at the backyard balcony in wait for her husband, Chad who was running from work due to some overtime work development that that caught up with him.

In her usual admiration to Leroy, at this time she noticed some strange and exciting feelings developing inside her as she watches this young Mandingo boy, Leroy over his total control of the lawn mower with macho, she began to imagine how he could transcend such to a woman such as her. It was like her whole tender body was tingling. She could feel every bead of sweat that trickled down Leroy's body due to his display of control and total maneuvering of the lawn mower with strength and energy. Hey! She kept quiet to enjoy the moment nature presented to her as she termed it.

Referencing the old saying, "The closer the warmer", Brenda made a swift decision to put in a request to Chad for Leroy be allowed occasional entry into the main building's rooms she and her husband, Chad occupies to help tidy up some areas, especially with regards to vacuuming and cleaning the floors and shoving of furniture and furnishings around to clean up some hard to ordinarily reach areas. And her assumed legitimate request was immediately honored without bias by her unsuspecting husband, Chad. Hence, Leroy was formally informed through his mom, Daniela accordingly. From time to time with Brenda watching Leroy in his performance of his duties even with her husband's presence in and around the house, she finds herself getting excited, intrigued, and aroused uncontrollably.

As the sexual innuendo from Brenda to this young boy grows, Leroy being a fast intuitive person began feeling such and so developing ideas that he could well climb this mountain as he could tell when Brenda's body was in a meltdown mode because he has gotten into inducing her to do so as he was remotely sending her thoughts and images that cause her head to spin and her inner body to weep.

These two people from two different life expectancies, happens to fill themselves with flirtatious maneuvering and probable over gestures as Leroy would continue to plant erotic thoughts in Brenda's mind as she began doing some little things as overly as to indicate so inviting to the young guy, Leroy into her as she got into some seductive moves like wearing her blouse half open to expose herself to Leroy, getting a better part of his attention. But Leroy would pretentiously turn around as if he were not paying attention. Sometimes, Brenda would have Leroy hold a ladder for her as she climbs up to look in the loft purposely without undies.

On this day, Brenda got bold with her layout plan to ask Leroy to take off his shirt". Hey! That shirt of yours is almost a rag, take it off" He did just as she said, and prior to her handing him a new shirt, she viciously glanced at his powerful chest, naturally defined stomach and strong arms as she pulled him to her body. Now Leroy has had enough of it as he musters courage to oblige her moves as he held her tightly, but gently to lay her down on the floor with her back as she wrapped herself around his strong and powerful arms. Leroy paused to look at her for a minute as he swings to action to plow her deeply until her body began to shake.

He rode her with reckless abandon, and vengeance bearing in mind with each stroke of what he had seen Chad do to his mother. He drove home the fact that it was revenge till he left her far spent and overwhelmed in weakness as she lay still, probably basking in glow…, The Phone Rings!

Chapter Twelve

ELIMINATING SLAVERY

For most part, the said second-generation slavery is self-inflicted. It is inappropriately induced and imposed by and from the wrong quarters, per bad choices and selfishness of leaders who do not "supposedly" understand and comprehend that their inexcusable bad leaderships and corrupt tendencies facilitates transfer of wealth from the powerless to a few powerful. Hence, creating unsafe haven and untold hardships that leads to numerous unbearable life situations and circumstances that translates to slavery and slavery related conditions. And the process of eliminating or eradicating this act must be initiated by leaders of 3rd world countries, especially African leaders with dedicated spirit of patriotism and selfless service to developing and creating sustainable opportunities in their various countries and economies, making the best out of their given resources abound.

Ghana we all know for instance; a country of African Continent is presently Africa's quintessential government excelling in its governmental leadership dispensations that has ushered in tremendous developments in every facet to be termed success. But, the billion-dollar question remains, for how long. But, for how long will these seen and recorded successes last in Ghana? How long can it be sustained for one unrefined, selfish, and myopic leader with his group emerge from their high-horse to sudden power grab as synonymous with African Nations to return the marvelous work to ashes without decorum in the name of yet another brain-drained African? The black race that learns to fight outsiders by first destroying each other internally and loses the main battle due to mistrust and untenability within ranks in line with common African saying, "When brothers fight themselves to death, strangers inherit their properties".

The greatest set back to the black race is the Blackman fueled by his intrinsic greed desire, rather than the assumed Whiteman in relation to early slavery. An average Whiteman is capitalist minded, not just for selfish purpose, but for the overall development and betterment of his country or people (Patriotism). So, the slave merchants' mission for opportunities in Africa was so enhanced by greedy African community leaders who embraced the merchants and escorted them to the hinter lands for peanut compensations and remunerations. Very pertinent to say, now there are no more White merchants terrorizing African continent for slavery, African leaders and politicians are now taking advantage of their own people in their gluttonous pursuit of wealth and riches at the undue expenses of their people, ostensibly.

It is quite so disheartening and mind bugging that in-spite of being the world's most natural resourceful continent, Africa remains the worlds' most impoverished continent due to sycophancy and self-aggrandizement of its leaders and politicians. And it is impossible to avoid mentioning where Africans as a people have been with scares and open wounds cursed and created by obnoxious leaders that continues threatening our existence and better life spectrum.

For posterity, it is very pertinent to say it is an act of essence as time is of the essence to redeem the black race of this continent of extraordinary diversity (National Geography, Wild) as expected of the leaders, and the time is, but now. Believing that in every adversary, nature provides extraordinary solutions and Africans as a people fervently look forward to such for as a race, in not losing faith of living within the will of life. Otherwise, may live outside the blessings of God.

Chapter Thirteen
TRIBUTE

Africa as the second largest Continent in the World after Asia with over 1.3b people is so endowed with countless and insurmountable mineral resources like gold, diamond, uranium, petroleum, gas, and a host of others, though the poorest, bewitched with bad leaderships, bribery, and corruption, which may be termed as total lack of patriotism to the demise of economic growth and development in the Continent.

Suffice to say, despite all odds it may be pertinent to recognize few notable African leaders of repute who are of late doing their ultimate best to positively initiate long awaited transformations as expected of them in their various individual Countries of the Continent.

JOHN POMBE MAGUFULE of beautiful East African Country of Tanzania, who came to power on November 5, 2015, and for about six years he has brought tremendous changes to Tanzania, making the Country one of the best in East Africa despite its large population of about 50m people. He started with promise of continuity from his predecessor which he smartly did in a very transformative manner. He also listed and reorganized some of the twenty pressing challenges he gathered from Tanzanian citizens during his campaign tours and meetings all through the Country which he requested his parliament to support. To work on his promises, he began by cutting government spending, barring unnecessary and unprofitable foreign travels by government official, dropping both foreign and domestic conference and meeting delegations from fifty to five officials, reduction of top government officials' salaries and allowances amongst other impressive measures. He registered significant development in combating corruption with introduction of Economic Corruption and Organized Crime Hight Court Division which has handled numerous cases of over four hundred in which over three hundred has already been determined. H boldly embarked on outstanding programs of infrastructure developments, making cities of Da es Salaam and Dodoma one of the best cities in Africa. Hence, making Tanzania a Country of high income earning of Africa, that earned him the nickname, "Bulldozer".

NANA AKUFOUR ADDO of West African Country of Ghana. For the short period of his tenure in office, Nana Addo has already stamped very enviable footprint of good leadership in Ghana which so far earned him the reputation of being one of the best African leaders of our time. He has established himself as, "Man of the people" with the establishment of free Secondary School education, commitment to Ghana development, and significantly reduced, if not eliminated corruption to earn him a high approval rating. Since his rule in Ghana, this West African has become a very peaceful Country, and one of the best Countries to transact business in Africa. It must not be left out that one of the features that makes Nana standout as notable African Leader is his call out to Neo-Colonialism. He does not miss any given opportunity to call out on any Western World's interference on African matters. President Nana Kufuor Addo is one leader all Africans should be proud of in all ramifications.

PAUL KAGAME of Rwanda who was a former Military leader turned Politician who came to power in 2000 as the 6th President of Rwanda is described by his people of Rwanda as the most impressive leader of their Country. After the genocide of Rwanda whereby the Hutus tried killing every Tutsi, he has been able to reunite the two ethnic groups by sharing Parliamentary and other key Government positions among the two groups. He is regarded as gender equality advocate as he has incorporated greatest number of women in key positions of his cabinet more than anyone else in the entire World. He has skyrocketed a war turn Country into almost economic miracle. His adopted educational program has generated one of the greatest literacy rates in Africa, also with high rate of tourism to the Country reaching to a pick in a Country its Capital City, Kigali currently ranked the cleanest City in Africa which are all because of his impressive infrastructural programs that has transformed to high economic growth rate.

DANNY FOURE of Seychelles, the thinnest African Country both in population and landmark. Though the smallest African Country, but by no means the least successful in the Continent.

Seychelles stands as the richest going by GDP per Capital. It is a tourist heaven and one of the best Countries to do business in Africa all by the able leadership of Danny Faure who was sworn into office in October 2016. He stands out as a strong fighter of corruption which has put him in the fore front of exemplary African leader among other attributes.

AHMED ABIY of Ethiopia who is one of the youngest African Leaders at a very youthful age of 44 years. The positive changes in Ethiopia have become so fast since Ahmed Abiy became the Prime Minister in April 2018. The reason he has already been awarded Noble Peace price in the first few Months of his coming to power, following the resignation of his predecessor, Hailemariam Desalegn. He started his good work by ending the Civil War between Ethiopia and Eritrea by agreeing to give up the disputed territory in his process of normalizing the long-expected relationship between Ethiopia and allied sister nation, Eritrea.

It may also be relevant and exciting to mention other up and coming African leaders such as MACKY SALL of Senegal, ADAMA BARROW of

Gambia, and MANUEL LOURENCO of Angola who are working tirelessly hard for their names to be included in the good book of great African leaders. As being reasoned by African Scholars, Civil Rights, and Social Justice advocates with excitement, the leadership of these few African leaders would help restore long awaited African pride, dignity, and economic development and growth that would help curtail, if not eradicate African migration. To these deserving few African leaders' impeccable initiatives and impressive results-oriented programs and leadership, we say, bravo!

World Mysteries

As we journey through the path of life, it is pertinent to pause as to wonder on some mysteries of this world we live in:

Taking a closer look at the 2018 FIFA World Tournament, I observed that the Month-long tournament which Started in the 6th Month and ended in the 7th Month of year 2018 had in its quarter final stage match pairings with some amazing and mind bugging facts or mysteries with the quarter finalists' country names in their match pairings as they randomly qualified from their various groups, thus.

France with 6-letter word pairs with Uruguay with 7-letter words

Brazil with 6-letter word pairs with Belgium with 7-letter words

Sweden with 6-letter word pairs with England with 7-letter words While,

Russia with 6-letter word pairs with Croatia with 7-letter words.

The mysteries continued with the quarter finals being played both on 6th and 7th days of the Month. Not to mention that the Championship game match was between France with 6-letter word and Croatia with 7-letter word which puts England at odd of qualifying for the Championship match.

I also wish to draw your kind attention to some other few mysteries as recorded in life:

> While the Christian worship place, CHURCH is a 6-letter word, the Moslem worship place, MOSQUE is also a 6-letter word.
> While the Christian book of worship, BIBLE is a 5-letter word, the Moslem book of worship, QURAN is a 5-letter word.
> While the word, LIFE is a 4-letter word, DEAD is having same 4-letter word.
> While LOVE is a 4-letter word, HATE is also a 4-letter word.
> While the word, FRIENDS has 7-letters, the word, ENEMIES also has 7-letters.
> While the word, POSITIVE has 8-letters, the word, NEGATIVE has same 8-letters.
> While SUCCESS comes up with 7-letters, FAILURE is same with 7-letters.

ABOVE indicates 5-letters, while BELOW matches it with same 5-letters.

The word, JOY is not left out with 3-letters, while SAD is same with 3-letters.

While the word, RIGHT has 5-letters, the opposite, WRONG is same with 5-letters.

While the word, HAPPY shows 5-letters, its opposite, ANGER is same with 5-letters.

The word, RICH with 4-letters pairs with POOR in the opposite with same 4-letters.

Then KNOWLEDGE showcases itself with 9-letter word so is IGNORANCE with same 9-letters.

And as you may discover, the list of life mysteries could be inexhaustible, and the good question remains, "What are behind these true-life mysteries?" Your wild guess is as good as mine!

Authorbiography

U.S. Citizen by naturalization, Nigerian by birth, Anelechi Bon Agoha is also author of the following two books: "Paid in Own Token" and "Your Destiny Is Your Choice".

In 2005, Anelechi Bon starred in a U.S. based African home-movie, "Far from Home". He studied Cardiovascular Technology at Sanford Brown Institute, Maryland, Criminal Justice at University of Maryland Global Campus, and Purchasing & Supply Management at the Federal Polytechnic, Owerri, Imo State, Nigeria. Anelechi Bon Agoha is a family-oriented man blessed with three incredible children.

www.ingramcontent.com/pod-product-compliance
Lightning Source LLC
LaVergne TN
LVHW040154080526
838202LV00042B/3157